BEHIND THE SCENES BIOGRAPHIES

WHAT YOU NEVER KNEW ABOUT SABRINA CARPENTER

by Mari Bolte

CAPSTONE PRESS
a capstone imprint

This is an unauthorized biography.

Published by Capstone Press, an imprint of Capstone
1710 Roe Crest Drive, North Mankato, Minnesota 56003
capstonepub.com

Library of Congress Cataloging-in-Publication Data
Names: Bolte, Mari, author.
Title: What you never knew about Sabrina Carpenter / by Mari Bolte.
Description: North Mankato, Minnesota : Capstone Press, 2026. | Series: Behind the scenes biographies | Includes bibliographical references and index. | Audience: Ages 9-11 | Audience: Grades 4-6 | Summary: "Sabrina Carpenter captivates audiences with her singing, dancing, and acting abilities, but how did she get her start? Who were her favorite childhood stars? What popular cartoon characters has she voiced? High-interest details and bold photos of her high-profile life will enthrall reluctant and striving readers, while carefully leveled text will leave them feeling confident"— Provided by publisher.
Identifiers: LCCN 2025013171 (print) | LCCN 2025013172 (ebook) | ISBN 9798875253478 (hardcover) | ISBN 9798875253423 (paperback) | ISBN 9798875253430 (pdf) | ISBN 9798875253447 (epub) | ISBN 9798875253454 (kindle edition)
Subjects: LCSH: Carpenter, Sabrina—Juvenile literature. | Singers—United States—Juvenile literature. | LCGFT: Biographies.
Classification: LCC ML3930.C2633 B65 2026 (print) | LCC ML3930.C2633 (ebook) | DDC 782.42164092 [B]—dc23/eng/20250401
LC record available at https://lccn.loc.gov/2025013171
LC ebook record available at https://lccn.loc.gov/2025013172

Editorial Credits
Editor: Mandy Robbins; Designer: Elijah Blue; Media Researcher: Rebekah Hubstenberger; Production Specialist: Tori Abraham

Image Credits
Alamy: Rodolfo Sassano, 15; Getty Images: Dave Kotinsky, 28, Dimitrios Kambouris, 6, Emma McIntyre, 22, Frazer Harrison, 4, 21, Gareth Cattermole, 9 (top left), John Shearer, 17, Jonathan Leibson/WireImage, 8, Lisa Lake, 12, Marc Piasecki, 5, Matt Winkelmeyer, cover, 9 (middle left), Michael Buckner/Variety, 11, Monica Schipper, 27, Noam Galai, 25; Shutterstock: ADragan, 14 (bottom left), Arnont48, 7, ChicagoPhotographer, 18, Daria Kriukovska, 24, Foxy Fox, 29, Illerlok_xolms (line designs), cover and throughout, Irina Yakimchuk, 19 (upper right), Julia Korobko, 26 (ice cream cone), mhatzapa, 20 (music scale), New Africa, 14 (bottom right), Olga_TG, 26 (rainbow), PHLD Luca, 20 (Beatles album), Ruslan Semichev, 19 (middle), Salomi art, 10, Stefano Chiacchiarini '74, 16, Timmary, 23

Printed and bound in China. 006459

TABLE OF CONTENTS

Words in **bold** are in the glossary.

SHORT N'
SWEET

Sabrina Carpenter is a singer and songwriter. She has opened for Taylor Swift and played at Coachella. She has acted on TV and in movies.

Sabrina is a style **icon**. She was invited to the Met Gala and Vogue World.

But what don't you know about Sabrina? Turn the page and find out!

POP STAR **QUIZ!**

1. **How many sisters does Sabrina have?**

   a) 2
   b) 3
   c) 4
   d) 5

2. **Sabrina's middle name is:**

   a) AnnLynn
   b) Analise
   c) Summer

3. Sabrina's first acting role was on:

a) *Sofia the First*
b) *Phineas and Ferb*
c) *Law & Order: Special Victims Unit*
d) *Girl Meets World*

4. Who did Sabrina sing with on *Saturday Night Live: The 50th Anniversary Special?*

a) Taylor Swift
b) Paul Simon
c) Paul McCartney

Answers:

1. b **2.** a **3.** c **4.** b

ON MY WAY

Young Sabrina loved watching *Hannah Montana*. In 2009, she entered a singing competition hosted by Miley Cyrus. It was called "Be a Star." Sabrina came in third out of 10,000 people. She was just 10 years old.

After the show, Sabrina started a YouTube channel. She sang **covers** of popular songs. Adele and Taylor Swift were two of her favorite singers.

Starting in 2012, Sabrina was on the Disney cartoon *Sofia the First*. She voiced Princess Vivian. Ariel Winter voiced Sofia. They are still friends.

Joey King is another of Sabrina's friends. They met at a **charity** event when they were 12. Sabrina was in Joey's wedding in 2023.

FACT

Sabrina's aunt is Emmy-award-winning voice actress Nancy Cartwright. Her most famous role is Bart Simpson from *The Simpsons*.

Joey King and Sabrina

Disney
Girl meets World
Maya Hart
Riley Matthews
girls 7-16

Another long-time friend was a Disney star too. Sabrina met Rowan Blanchard on the set of *Girl Meets World* in 2013. Rowan and Sabrina recorded the show's **theme song** together. "Take On the World" made Billboard's Kids Digital Song Sales **chart**.

FACT

Sabrina was in *Mean Girls* on Broadway in 2020. The play was shut down due to COVID after two nights.

LOOKING AT ME

Sabrina first went on tour in 2016. The EVOLution Tour traveled across the United States. VIP fans got to hang out with Sabrina before the show at a french fry party. Sabrina also loves chicken fajitas. She eats chocolate cake in every city she visits!

Sabrina is a long-time Swiftie. Her favorite albums are *1989*, *Folklore*, and *Midnights*. She went to her first Taylor Swift concert at 10 years old. The two singers met in 2017 and became friends. In 2023 and 2024, Sabrina opened for Taylor's Eras Tour.

SHE'S WORKING LATE

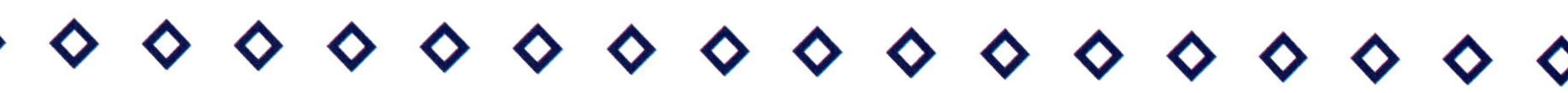

On April 11, 2024, "Espresso" was released as a **single**. It was from Sabrina's album *Short n' Sweet*. The next day, she sang "Espresso" at the Coachella music festival. For 14 weeks, it was one of the top three songs on the Billboard Top 100.

FACT

In 2024, fans in New York, Chicago, and Hollywood got to visit Short n' Sweet **pop-up** cafes. There were themed treats, special merchandise, and photo opportunities.

Sabrina's next singles were "Taste" and "Please Please Please." They joined "Espresso" on the charts. They were songs two, three, and four on the list. It was the first time a solo artist had their first three singles in the top five slots at the same time. The only group to ever do this was the Beatles!

The Beatles' *Abbey Road* album cover

"It's an hour of literal nonsense."

—Sabrina Carpenter on her Netflix Christmas special

Sabrina loves Christmas. Her holiday album, *Fruitcake*, came out in 2023. *A Nonsense Christmas with Sabrina Carpenter* came out on Netflix the next year.

Fame is not always fun. Sabrina is open about her **anxiety**. She talks about it publicly.

TAKE ON THE WORLD

Sabrina met Ryan Seacrest in 2014. She became an **ambassador** for the Ryan Seacrest Foundation two years later. She visits children's hospitals and talks to patients. She plays games with them and sings. Sabrina tells kids that they're never too young to follow their dreams.

In 2020, Sabrina raised money for Doctors Without Borders. She has supported World Cancer Day too. She also helped with the Palestine Children's Relief Fund.

In 2024, she worked with an ice cream company. They raised money for the Ali Forney Center. The **nonprofit** helps protect LGBTQIA+ youth.

MGM

The Sabrina Carpenter Fund supports local organizations. Mental health and animals are two issues Sabrina cares about. The LGBTQIA+ community is another. In less than two months, the fund had raised nearly $600,000.

$600,000

Glossary

ambassador (am-BA-suh-duhr)—a person who represents a group or organization

anxiety (ang-ZYE-uh-tee)—a feeling of worry or fear

charity (CHAYR-uh-tee)—a group that raises money or collects goods to help people in need

chart (CHART)—a ranking of the most popular songs and albums in the United States

cover (KUH-ver)—a new recording or performance of a song originally done by someone else

icon (EYE-kahn)—someone who is honored and respected

nonprofit (non-PRAH-fit)—a group that gives all of the money it raises to help a cause

pop-up (POP-up)—a store or business that opens quickly in a temporary location

single (SING-guhl)—one song from an album; often played on the radio to get a new album noticed

theme song (THEEM SONG)—music that is typically played at the start of a TV show or other program

Read More

Connors, Kathleen. *Sabrina Carpenter.* Buffalo, New York: Enslow Publishing, 2025.

Klepeis, Alicia Z. *Taylor Swift: Music Industry Leader.* Minneapolis: Abdo Publishing, a division of ABDO, 2025.

Schuh, Mari. *What You Never Know About Ariana Grande.* North Mankato, MN: Capstone, 2023.

Internet Sites

19 Facts You Didn't Know About Sabrina Carpenter
iheart.com/content/2018-05-10-facts-you-didnt-know-about-sabrina-carpenter/

Billboard: Sabrina Carpenter
billboard.com/artist/sabrina-carpenter/

Biography: Sabrina Carpenter
biography.com/musicians/a62488913/sabrina-carpenter

Index

About the Author

Mari Bolte is the author and editor of hundreds of children's books. Every book is her favorite book as long as readers learned something and enjoyed themselves!